MUSICAL INSTRUMENTS OF THE WORLD

Brass and Woodwind

M. J. Knight

W
FRANKLIN WATTS
LONDON•SYDNEY

 An Appleseed Editions book

First published in 2005 by Franklin Watts
96 Leonard Street, London, EC2A 4XD

Franklin Watts Australia
45-51 Huntley Street, Alexandria, NSW 2015

© 2005 Appleseed Editions

Created by Appleseed Editions Ltd,
Well House, Friars Hill, Guestling, East Sussex, TN35 4ET

Designed by Helen James

ISBN 0 7496 5844 4

A CIP catalogue for this book is available from the British Library.

Photographs by Corbis (Dave Bartruff, Bohemian Nomad Picturemakers, Joseph Sohm;
ChromoSohm Inc., PITCHAL FREDERIC/CORBIS SYGMA, THE SCOTSMAN/CORBIS
SYGMA, Freelance Consulting Services Pty Ltd, Franz-Marc Frei, Philip Gould, Chris
Hellier, Robert Holmes, Hulton-Deutsch Collection, Wolfgang Kaehler, David Katzenstein,
Michael Keller, Lawrence Manning, Stephanie Maze, Roger Ressmeyer, Reuters,
Royalty-Free, Anders Ryman, Phil Schermeister, Ariel Skelley, Paul A. Souders)

Printed in Thailand

Contents

Introducing Brass and woodwind instruments

This book is about the musical instruments that belong to the brass and woodwind families.

The instruments in these families create a sound when the air inside them vibrates. Brass players press their lips to the mouthpiece of their instrument and blow hard down it to create notes. Most woodwind players blow into a piece of cane in the mouthpiece, called a reed, to make notes.

The sound each instrument makes depends on how long it is. The longer the instrument, the lower the notes it plays.

You can see from the faces of these musicians how much they enjoy performing. They are playing at a concert in Paris.

The first woodwind instruments were all made of wood, but today some, such as the saxophone, are made of metal. Brass instruments were so-called because they were made of a metal called brass.

You can hear many of these instruments playing classical music in an orchestra. The woodwind section usually includes flutes, clarinets, oboes, bassoons and sometimes a saxophone. The brass section has French horns, trumpets, trombones and a tuba.

Today many of these instruments also play other types of music, including folk, rock, pop and jazz.

This brass band is marching along the streets of Pasadena in California as it plays. Look for the plumes on some of their hats.

The first horns

The first horns The first horns

Musical horns were first made from animal horns, with a hole pierced at the narrow end. In Africa these were antelope horns. They were used to send signals.

One of the oldest types of horn is the shofar, or ram's horn. This is still played in Jewish ceremonies today.

Hundreds of years ago, huntsmen blew horns to signal to each other during stag or fox hunts. The post-horn grew up from these hunting horns during the 1400s. It was sounded by postmen when they arrived and departed.

The bugle is a coiled horn which was played by soldiers and watchmen from the 1700s.

From these beginnings came the horns we hear today.

The master of the hunt blows his hunting horn to signal to other members of the fox hunt. He wears a traditional red jacket.

French horn

French horn

French horn

French horn French horn

This French horn player is pressing down two of the three valves on his horn with his left hand to make the right note.

This horn is made from a coiled metal tube with a wide cone shape, called the bell, at one end. It plays an important part in orchestras and brass bands today.

French horn players put one hand inside the bell to play. They push their lips hard into the mouthpiece and blow. They can make different notes by changing the shape of their lips. The French horn also has three small levers, called valves, which players press to make different notes.

Did you know?
If you pulled a French horn out straight, it would be nearly 9 metres long.

Trumpet Trumpet Trumpet

The trumpet is a very old instrument. Silver and bronze trumpets were played by the Ancient Egyptians thousands of years ago. Trumpets have been played since then by the Greeks, the Romans and in countries all over Europe.

Today's trumpets are tightly-coiled metal tubes, with a mouthpiece at one end. At the other end is a cone called the bell.

Trumpet players push down three small buttons called valves to make different notes. Trumpets make a bright, lively sound.

Did you know?

The Greeks compared the sound of the trumpet to that of an elephant. Today elephants are still said to trumpet through their trunks.

These students are learning to play the trumpet on the island of Haiti in the Caribbean.

8

Trombone

Trombone Trombone Trombone Trombone

Troy Andrews blows his hardest into his trombone as he plays with his brother in a jazz cafe in New Orleans, Louisiana, USA.

The long metal tube of the trombone is curled round twice. It has a section called the slide, which the player can move in and out to create different notes.

The trombone plays lower notes than the trumpet, because the tube it is made from is longer. It is one of the loudest instruments in an orchestra, but can also be played very softly.

The trombone was first played around 600 years ago. In England, its first name was the sackbut.

Tuba

Tuba Tuba

Grand-daddy of all the brass instruments is the tuba, which plays the lowest notes. It is so big that you have to sit down and rest the tuba on your knee to play it.

The biggest tuba is 2.4 metres high, which makes it taller than the person playing it. If the tube of this tuba was uncoiled, it would be almost 14 metres long.

The low notes of a tuba sound warm and deep when you hear it playing in an orchestra or brass band. You need a lot of breath to play a tuba.

A tuba player presses his lips tightly into the mouthpiece to make a note. He changes the shape of his lips to make different notes.

Sousaphone

An American called John Philip Sousa invented the sousaphone about 100 years ago. He wanted a low-sounding brass instrument to play in marching bands.

The sousaphone has a very deep sound. It is so big that the sousaphone player has to carry it looped around him, with part of it resting on his left shoulder.

Small buttons called valves open and close parts of the tube to make different notes.

Brass sousaphones are very heavy, so modern ones are often made from fibreglass.

You have to be strong and have a lot of breath to play the sousaphone. This player is part of a band in New Orleans, Louisiana, USA.

Conch Conch Conch Conch Conch

Thousands of years ago, someone found an empty shell with a broken tip, put it to his lips, and blew a note through it. He had played a conch shell trumpet.

The conch has been played ever since in countries around the Pacific Ocean, from Mexico to Polynesia.

The shell sounds only one note, but it is loud enough to carry over a long distance. It has been blown by soldiers to frighten their enemies, and by farmers to call workers from the fields. Today the conch is played at religious festivals.

A boy from the Cook Islands in the South Pacific Ocean performs during a festival.

Didjeridu

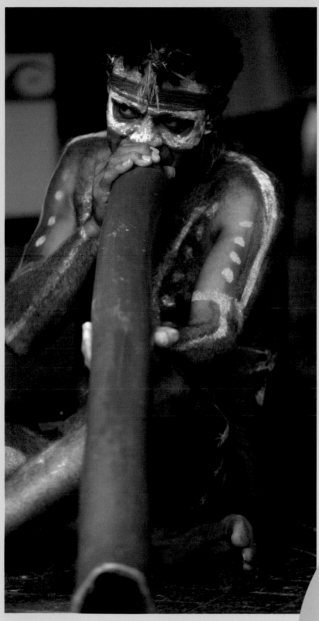

The didjeridu is a traditional Australian instrument, made from the branch of a eucalyptus tree. The branch must be at least 7.5 centimetres wide, 1.2 metres long, and hollow.

To play the didjeridu, you blow into one end. Each didjeridu can play only one note, but players move their lips and use their voices to make the note sound in different ways.

Didjeridus accompany traditional singing and dancing. They are also played in some Australian pop bands.

David Kennedy wears Aboriginal face and body paint to play his didjeridu in Sydney, Australia.

Did you know?

Insects called termites hollow out tree branches while the tree is still standing. A didjeridu builder peels off the tree bark and taps the wood with his knuckles. The sound tells him whether the tree is solid or hollow.

Didjeridu

Oboe Oboe Oboe

Bright, sweet notes come from the oboe's long, thin shape. The first oboes were invented to replace the shawm, which was a type of pipe. The shawm made a harsh, buzzing sound and could only be played outside.

Oboe players blow through a double reed, which is made from two small slices of cane tied tightly together. They cover the finger holes and press the keys to create different notes.

These oboe players are practising for a performance with their band at Oregon State University, USA.

Oboes play mainly classical music in orchestras and ensembles.

Cor anglais

Cor anglais

Cor anglais is French for English horn, but no-one knows how it got its name, as it is not a horn, nor is it English. It is a member of the oboe family, and plays lower notes than the oboe, making a soft, sad sound.

The cor anglais has a curved brass tube at the top called a crook, which holds the reed. The lower end is egg-shaped and is called the bell. This creates the velvety sound made by the cor anglais.

The instrument has finger holes covered by small metal caps called keys.

This musician is sitting in a boat, waiting to play her cor anglais to whales in a bay in Mexico.

15

Clarinet Clarinet Clarinet

The shrill, sweet sound of the clarinet was first heard in the early 1700s. Today clarinets play both classical music and jazz.

Like other wind instruments, the clarinet is played through a reed, made from a piece of cane. A clarinet-player can change the sound of a note by moving her mouth to change the vibrations made by the reed.

The clarinet also has finger holes and metal keys, which create different notes.

There are several different types of clarinet, and the soprano clarinet is the one most often played.

These clarinet players carry their music clipped to their instruments. They are part of a marching jazz band in Norway.

Bassoon Bassoon

A bassoon player holds the reed tightly in his mouth and blows through it to make a note.

Did you know?

You can make your own reed from a blade of grass. Hold it flat between the sides of your thumbs and blow hard on it to make a loud, harsh note.

The clown of the woodwind instruments, the bassoon, plays the lowest notes. It is a doubled-up wooden tube with a curved metal tube called a crook, which holds the reed. The crook makes it easier for players to blow through the mouthpiece and press down the keys at the same time.

Bassoonists wear their instrument on a neck strap when they play. The bassoon is most often heard in an orchestra.

Saxophone Saxophone

The metal saxophone is really a woodwind instrument. A Belgian instrument-maker called Adolphe Sax invented it about 150 years ago.

The saxophone is a tube of thin metal, which widens at one end into a cone shape. It has 18-21 finger holes, covered with small metal keys. A reed made from cane is fixed to the mouthpiece. The vibrations made by the reed create the notes. The sound of the saxophone is smooth and rich.

The smallest saxophone plays the highest notes and is called a sopranino. The largest is a contrabass. The most popular saxophones are the tenor and alto.

Did you know?

The most valuable saxophone in the world was sold for $144,500 in London in 1994. The saxophone had belonged to a famous jazz musician called Charlie 'Bird' Parker.

You can see how this jazz musician presses down the metal keys on his saxophone to play the notes.

Brass and woodwind in jazz

Many brass and woodwind instruments play jazz. This style of music grew up in America from work songs and spirituals sung by people from Africa.

It was first called jazz in the late 1800s, and its home was New Orleans in Louisiana. In jazz each instrument plays its own tune and the musicians often improvise.

Jazz music spread through America during the 1900s. In the 1920s jazz musicians came to Europe and jazz began to spread all over the world. There are many different types of jazz, including Dixieland, swing, bebop, traditional and free jazz.

Members of the Preservation Hall Jazz Band playing in New Orleans, the home of jazz.

Mouth organ

Mouth organ Mouth organ Mouth organ

The mouth organ is also called the harmonica. It is a metal box with a row of reeds inside, which sound when you blow or suck on them. Harmonicas were first made about 150 years ago in Germany.

Some folk singers play the harmonica at the same time as the guitar. The harmonica is held in a metal frame around the singer's neck, so his hands are free to play the guitar.

This musician is a one-man band. As well as the harmonica, he plays the guitar, and has a drum and cymbal strapped to his back.

Sheng
Sheng Sheng Sheng

Thousands of years before the mouth organ was invented Chinese musicians were playing the sheng.

The sheng is made from 17 bamboo pipes and a gourd (a fruit like a small pumpkin). The pipes are held together with a metal band. Each one has a finger hole and a reed, which vibrates when the finger hole is covered.

Sheng players blow and suck air through the mouthpiece, while covering the finger holes to make different notes. Shengs are often played in Chinese orchestras today.

A sheng player in traditional dress plays the pipes at a festival in Yunnan, China.

Bagpipes

Bagpipes Bagpipes Bagpipes Bagpipes

Bagpipes have a bag of air with several pipes sticking out of it. They are played in many countries, including Scotland, England, Ireland, France, Italy, Greece, India and countries of Eastern Europe.

Traditional dress for Scottish bagpipers is a tartan kilt, a dark jacket and a sporran around the waist.

22

The Scottish bagpipes make a loud, wailing sound, which carries a long distance in the open air. The bagpiper blows into a long pipe called a blowpipe to fill the bag with air. He has to keep blowing to make sure the bag stays full.

The air escapes through the other pipes. Several large pipes called drones play only one note, while a small pipe called the chanter plays the tune. The chanter has finger holes that the piper covers to make different notes. The sound made by bagpipes is called a skirl.

This piper is covering the holes of the chanter pipe to make different notes. You can see the bag full of air under his elbow.

In southern Italy, bagpipes called zampogna are played in the streets of Naples at Christmas-time, to serenade images of baby Jesus.

Did you know?

Bagpipes were first made by shepherds from the skins and bones of sheep and goats about 5,000 years ago.

Alghaita Alghaita Alghaita

Folk musicians in Nigeria play a wooden pipe called the alghaita. It grew up from the shawm, a type of pipe which made a harsh, buzzing sound.

The alghaita has a metal mouthpiece and a wooden body which is covered in leather.

The player presses his lips to the disc above the mouthpiece and puffs out his cheeks to play. The air in his cheeks allows him to play continuously, without stopping to take a breath. He makes different notes by covering the finger holes.

A Nigerian alghaita player puffs out his cheeks to make a loud sound.

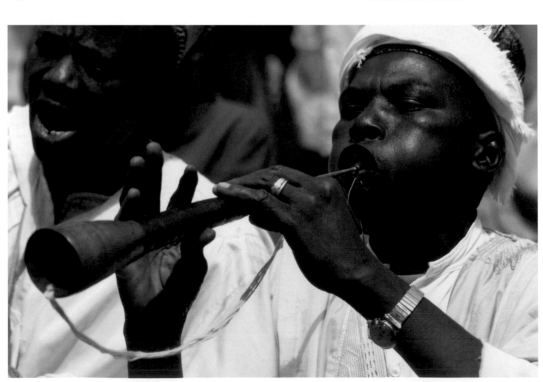

Alphorn Alphorn Alphorn

The alphorn is a very long, hollow instrument, made from wood. The first alphorns were made from the trunks of fallen trees.

The hard rockface of the Swiss mountain helps to bounce the sound made by this alphorn player into the next valley.

An alphorn can be 3 metres long, and has to be played standing up. The player stands at one end and rests the upturned end on the ground.

Herdsmen in the Swiss Alps have played alphorns to signal to each other for hundreds of years. The sound is like a groaning cow, and it carries over long distances in the mountains.

Did you know?

The longest alphorn ever built was nearly 24 metres long. It was built by a man called Peter Wutherich, who lived in Idaho.

25

Tiktiri Tiktiri Tiktiri Tiktiri Tiktiri

The tiktiri is an Indian instrument like a double clarinet. It is made from a gourd (a round, pumpkin-like fruit), with two cane pipes coming out of it.

One of the pipes plays only one note. The other has finger holes, which the tiktiri player covers to make different notes while blowing into the mouthpiece.

Tiktiris make a whining sound and are traditionally played by snake charmers.

An Indian snake charmer plays his tiktiri.

Concertina

Concertina Concertina

Concertinas have two hexagonal (six-sided) end pieces, joined by folded bellows. The concertina player holds one end in each hand and presses the bellows in and out to make the air move inside.

Tiny strips of metal inside vibrate when the air moves across them to make the concertina sound. To play a tune, the concertina player presses buttons on both ends of the instrument at the same time as moving the bellows in and out.

The sound made by a concertina is wheezy and loud and it is often played at open-air concerts.

Walter Jagiello comes from Miami, USA. His nickname is The Polka King because he loves to play this folk dance music.

27

Zurna Zurna Zurna Zurna Zurna Zurna Zurna

The zurna is a carved wooden pipe from Turkey, which is sometimes decorated with silver. It grew up from the shawm, a type of pipe which made a harsh, buzzing sound when played.

The zurna player blows through a double reed, made from two small pieces of cane, to make the notes. The sound made by the zurna is loud and buzzing.

Zurnas are played in folk bands at festivals and weddings in Turkey.

A Turkish man plays his zurna loudly as he walks in a festival procession.

This amazing-looking instrument was invented in France four hundred years ago.

The serpent's body is a long wooden tube, moulded into a double-S shape. The tube is covered in leather to make it look like a real serpent. It has two sets of finger holes, three for the left hand and three for the right.

The player blows into the cup-shaped mouthpiece to create a sound. The serpent is played upright or held at right angles to the player's body.

This serpent is being played by a soldier about 60 years ago. Today you can see serpents in museums.

29

Words to remember

accompany To play alongside a singer, or another musician who is playing the tune.

bell The wide end of a brass or woodwind instrument. The bell is often cone-shaped.

bellows Part of an instrument which holds air. When the bellows are squeezed, the instrument makes a sound.

brass band A group of musicians who play brass instruments together with percussion instruments, such as drums and cymbals.

classical music Serious music is sometimes called classical music to separate it from popular music. Classical music can also mean music which was written during the late 18th and early 19th centuries and followed certain rules.

crook A thin tube on some long instruments which helps players reach all the finger holes.

ensemble A small group of musicians who play together.

fibreglass A lightweight material made from glass.

finger holes The holes in an instrument which the player has to cover to make different notes.

folk music Traditional songs and tunes that are so old that no one remembers who wrote them.

improvise To invent the tune you are playing as you play it. This skill is mainly used in jazz music.

jazz A type of music played by a group of instruments in which each one plays its own tune. Jazz musicians often improvise, or make up, the tunes they play.

keys Small metal caps on a woodwind instrument which cover finger holes.

mouthpiece The part of a brass or woodwind instrument which the player puts in his or her mouth and blows through.

musician Someone who plays an instrument or sings.

orchestra A group of about 90 musicians playing classical music together.

pop music Popular music which is entertaining and easy to listen to.

reed A small, thin piece of cane or metal in the mouthpiece of some wind instruments which vibrates to make a note.

rock music Pop music with a strong beat, or rhythm.

spiritual A type of religious song which began among black slaves in the southern United States more than 200 years ago.

valves Small buttons or levers on a brass instrument which the player can press to make different notes.

vibrate To move up and down very quickly, or quiver. A reed vibrates when air passes over it.

Index